Learn Spanish with The Novel La Cruz Del Diablo

HypLern Interlinear Project
www.hyplern.com

First edition: 2025, October

Author: Gustavo Adolfo Becquer
Translation: Kees van den End
Foreword: Camilo Andrés Bonilla Carvajal PhD

ISBN: 978-1-988830-83-4

kees@hyplern.com
www.hyplern.com

Learn Spanish with The Novel La Cruz Del Diablo

Interlinear Spanish to English

Author
Gustavo Adolfo Becquer

Translation
Kees van den End

HypLern Interlinear Project
www.hyplern.com

The HypLern Method

Learning a foreign language should not mean leafing through page after page in a bilingual dictionary until one's fingertips begin to hurt. Quite the contrary, through everyday language use, friendly reading, and direct exposure to the language we can get well on our way towards mastery of the vocabulary and grammar needed to read native texts. In this manner, learners can be successful in the foreign language without too much study of grammar paradigms or rules. Indeed, Seneca expresses in his sixth epistle that "Longum iter est per praecepta, breve et efficax per exempla[1]."

The HypLern series constitutes an effort to provide a highly effective tool for experiential foreign language learning. Those who are genuinely interested in utilizing original literary works to learn a foreign language do not have to use conventional graded texts or adapted versions for novice readers. The former only distort the actual essence of literary works, while the latter are highly reduced in vocabulary and relevant content. This collection aims to bring the lively experience of reading stories as directly told by their very authors to foreign language learners.

Most excited adult language learners will at some point seek their teachers' guidance on the process of learning to read in the foreign language rather than seeking out external opinions. However, both teachers and learners lack a general reading technique or strategy. Oftentimes, students undertake the reading task equipped with nothing more than a bilingual dictionary, a grammar book, and lots of courage. These efforts often end in frustration as the student builds mis-constructed nonsensical sentences after many hours spent on an aimless translation drill.

Consequently, we have decided to develop this series of interlinear translations intended to afford a comprehensive edition of unabridged texts. These texts are presented as they were originally written with no changes in word choice or order. As a result, we have a translated piece conveying the true meaning under every word from the original work. Our readers receive then two books in just one volume: the original version and its translation.

The reading task is no longer a laborious exercise of patiently decoding unclear and seemingly complex paragraphs. What's more, reading becomes an enjoyable and meaningful process of cultural, philosophical and linguistic learning. Independent learners can then acquire expressions and vocabulary while understanding pragmatic and socio-cultural dimensions of the target language by reading in it rather than reading about it.

Our proposal, however, does not claim to be a novelty. Interlinear translation is as old as the Spanish tongue, e.g. "glosses of [Saint] Emilianus", interlinear bibles in Old German, and of course James Hamilton's work in the 1800s. About the latter, we remind the readers, that as a revolutionary freethinker he promoted the publication of Greco-Roman classic works and further pieces in diverse languages. His effort, such as ours, sought to lighten the exhausting task of looking words up in large glossaries as an educational practice: "if there is any thing which fills reflecting men with melancholy and regret, it is the waste of mortal time, parental money, and puerile happiness, in the present method of pursuing Latin and Greek[2]".

Additionally, another influential figure in the same line of thought as Hamilton was John Locke. Locke was also the philosopher and translator of the Fabulae AEsopi in an interlinear plan. In 1600, he was already suggesting that interlinear texts, everyday communication, and use of the target language could be the most appropriate ways to achieve language learning:

> ...the true and genuine Way, and that which I would propose, not only as the easiest and best, wherein a Child might, without pains or Chiding, get a Language which others are wont to be whipt for at School six or seven Years together...[3]

---

1 "The journey is long through precepts, but brief and effective through examples". Seneca, Lucius Annaeus. (1961) Ad Lucilium Epistulae Morales, vol. I. London: W. Heinemann.

2 In: Hamilton, James (1829?) History, principles, practice and results of the Hamiltonian system, with answers to the Edinburgh and Westminster reviews; A lecture delivered at Liverpool; and instructions for the use of the books published on the system. Londres: W. Aylott and Co., 8, Pater Noster Row. p. 29.

3 In: Locke, John. (1693) Some thoughts concerning education. Londres: A. and J. Churchill. pp. 196-7.

Who can benefit from this edition?

We identify three kinds of readers, namely, those who take this work as a search tool, those who want to learn a language by reading authentic materials, and those attempting to read writers in their original language. The HypLern collection constitutes a very effective instrument for all of them.

1. For the first target audience, this edition represents a search tool to connect their mother tongue with that of the writer's. Therefore, they have the opportunity to read over an original literary work in an enriching and certain manner.
2. For the second group, reading every word or idiomatic expression in its actual context of use will yield a strong association between the form, the collocation, and the context. This will have a direct impact on long term learning of passive vocabulary, gradually building genuine reading ability in the original language. This book is an ideal companion not only to independent learners but also to those who take lessons with a teacher. At the same time, the continuous feeling of achievement produced during the process of reading original authors both stimulates and empowers the learner to study[1].
3. Finally, the third kind of reader will notice the same benefits as the previous ones. The proximity of a word and its translation in our interlinear texts is a step further from other collections, such as the Loeb Classical Library. Although their works might be considered the most famous in this genre, the presentation of texts on opposite pages hinders the immediate link between words and their semantic equivalence in our native tongue (or one we have a strong mastery of).

---

1 Some further ways of using the present work include:

1. As you progress through the stories, focus less on the lower line (the English translation). Instead, try to read through the upper line, staying in the foreign language as long as possible.
2. Even if you find glosses or explanatory footnotes about the mechanics of the language, you should make your own hypotheses on word formation and syntactical functions in a sentence. Feel confident about inferring your own language rules and test them progressively. You can also take notes concerning those idiomatic expressions or special language usage that calls your attention for later study.
3. As soon as you finish each text, check the reading in the original version (with no interlinear or parallel translation). This will fulfil the main goal of this

collection: bridging the gap between readers and original literary works, training them to read directly and independently.

Why interlinear?

Conventionally speaking, tiresome reading in tricky and exhausting circumstances has been the common definition of learning by texts. This collection offers a friendly reading format where the language is not a stumbling block anymore. Contrastively, our collection presents a language as a vehicle through which readers can attain and understand their authors' written ideas.

While learning to read, most people are urged to use the dictionary and distinguish words from multiple entries. We help readers skip this step by providing the proper translation based on the surrounding context. In so doing, readers have the chance to invest energy and time in understanding the text and learning vocabulary; they read quickly and easily like a skilled horseman cantering through a book.

Thereby we stress the fact that our proposal is not new at all. Others have tried the same before, coming up with evident and substantial outcomes. Certainly, we are not pioneers in designing interlinear texts. Nonetheless, we are nowadays the only, and doubtless, the best, in providing you with interlinear foreign language texts.

Handling instructions

Using this book is very easy. Each text should be read at least three times in order to explore the whole potential of the method. The first phase is devoted to comparing words in the foreign language to those in the mother tongue. This is to say, the upper line is contrasted to the lower line as the following example shows:

Yo	no	pude	menos	de	sonreír.
I	not	could	less	of	smile
				(than)	

The second phase of reading focuses on capturing the meaning and sense of the original text. As readers gain practice with the method, they should be able to focus on the target language without getting distracted by the translation. New users of the method, however, may find it helpful to cover the translated lines with a piece of paper as illustrated in the image below. Subsequently, they try to understand the meaning of every word, phrase, and entire sentences in the target language itself, drawing on the translation only when necessary. In this phase, the reader should resist the temptation to look at the translation for every word. In doing so, they will find that they are able to understand a good portion of the text by reading directly in the target language, without the crutch of the translation. This is the skill we are looking to train: the ability to read and understand native materials and enjoy them as native speakers do, that being, directly in the original language.

Yo no pude menos de   sonreír.
I   not could l

In the final phase, readers will be able to understand the meaning of the text when reading it without additional help. There may be some less common words and phrases which have not cemented themselves yet in the reader's brain, but the majority of the story should not pose any problems. If desired, the reader can use an SRS or some other memorization method to learning these straggling words.

Yo no pude menos de sonreír.

Above all, readers will not have to look every word up in a dictionary to read a text in the foreign language. This otherwise wasted time will be spent concentrating on their principal interest. These new readers will tackle authentic texts while learning their vocabulary and expressions to use in further communicative (written or oral) situations. This book is just one work from an overall series with the same purpose. It really helps those who are afraid of having "poor vocabulary" to feel confident about reading directly in the language. To all of them and to all of you, welcome to the amazing experience of living a foreign language!

Additional tools

Check out shop.hyplern.com or contact us at info@hyplern.com for free mp3s (if available) and free empty (untranslated) versions of the eBooks that we have on offer.

For some of the older eBooks and paperbacks we have Windows, iOS and Android apps available that, next to the interlinear format, allow for a pop-up format, where hovering over a word or clicking on it gives you its meaning. The apps also have any mp3s, if available, and integrated vocabulary practice.

Visit the site hyplern.com for the same functionality online. This is where we will be working non-stop to make all our material available in multiple formats, including audio where available, and vocabulary practice.

Table of Contents

Chapter   Page

1 - LA CRUZ DEL DIABLO - I   1

2 - LA CRUZ DEL DIABLO - II   15

3 - LA CRUZ DEL DIABLO - III   36

4 - LA CRUZ DEL DIABLO - IV   66

5 - LAS HOJAS SECAS   101

LA CRUZ DEL DIABLO - I

LA CRUZ DEL DIABLO
The Cross Of The Devil

Que lo creas o no, me importa bien poco.
That it (you) believe or not me (it) is important well little
Whether you believe it or not I don't care

Mi abuelo se lo narró a mi padre; mi
My grandfather -himself- it narrated to my father my
(told)

padre me lo ha referido a mí, y yo te lo
father me it has referred to me and I (to) you it
(related)

cuento ahora, siquiera no sea más que por pasar
tell now certainly not (it) be more than for to pass

el rato.
the while
(time)

I

El crepúsculo comenzaba a extender sus ligeras
The dusk started to extend its light

alas de vapor sobre las pintorescas orillas del
wings of vapor over the picturesque banks of the

Segre, cuando después de una fatigosa jornada
Segre (river) when after of a tiring journey

llegamos a Bellver, término de nuestro viaje.
(we) arrived to Bellver end of our trip

Bellver es una pequeña población situada a la
Bellver is a small village situated at the

falda de una colina, por detrás de la cual
slope of a hill -for- after of -the- which

se ven elevarse, como las gradas de un
-themselves- see rise itself like the steps of a
can be seen to rise

colosal anfiteatro de granito, las empinadas y
huge amphitheater of granite the tips and

nebulosas crestas de los Pirineos.
nebulous (mountain) tops of the Pyrenees

Los blancos caseríos que la rodean, salpicados
The white homesteads that it encircle splashed

aquí y allá sobre una ondulante sábana de
here and there over a undulating sheet of

verdura, parecen a lo lejos un bando de
green seem at the distance a band of
(flock)

palomas que han abatido su vuelo para apagar
doves that have interrupted their flight for to smother

su sed en las aguas de la ribera.
their thirst in the waters of the (river) bank

Una pelada roca, a cuyos pies tuercen éstas su
A bare rock at which feet twist these their

curso, y sobre cuya cima se notan aún
course and over which top themselves note still
are noted

remotos vestigios de construcción, señala la
distant vestiges of construction signaled the

antigua línea divisoria entre el condado de Urgel
old line dividing between the county of Urgel

y el más importante de sus feudos.
and the most important of its fiefs

A la derecha del tortuoso sendero que conduce
At the right of the tortuous path that leads

a este punto, remontando la corriente del río,
to this point ascending the stream of the river

y siguiendo sus curvas y frondosas márgenes,
and following its curves and leafy margins

se encuentra una cruz.
itself encounters a cross
    is located

El asta y los brazos son de hierro; la redonda
The shaft and the arms are from iron the round

base en que se apoya, de mármol, y la
base in that itself (it) supports of marble and the

escalinata que a ella conduce, de obscuros y
staircase that to her conducts from dark and

mal unidos fragmentos de sillería.
badly united fragments of ashlar
                             {large square stone}

La destructora acción de los años, que ha
The destructive action of the years that has

cubierto de orín el metal, ha roto y carcomido
covered of rust the metal has broken and rotten

la piedra de este monumento, entre cuyas
the stone of this monument between which

hendiduras crecen algunas plantas trepadoras que
indentations grow some plants climbers that
(cracks) creeper vines

suben enredándose hasta coronarlo, mientras una
rise tangling themselves until to crown it while an
(getting tangled)

vieja y corpulenta encina le sirve de dosel.
old and corpulent holm oak it serves of canopy
(as)

Yo había adelantado algunos minutos a mis
I had advanced some minutes to my
(gotten ahead)

compañeros de viaje, y deteniendo mi escuálida
companions of travel and stopping my squalid
traveling companions

cabalgadura, contemplaba en silencio aquella cruz,
horseback contemplated in silence that cross
(horse)

muda y sencilla expresión de las creencias y la
mute and simple expression of the beliefs and the

piedad de otros siglos.
piety of other centuries

Un mundo de ideas se agolpó a mi imaginación
A world of ideas itself crowded to my imagination

en aquel instante. Ideas ligerísimas, sin forma
in that instant Ideas very light without form

determinada, que unían entre sí, como
determined that (they) united between each other like

un invisible hilo de luz, la profunda soledad de
an invisible thread of light the deep loneliness of

aquellos lugares, el alto silencio de la naciente
those places the high silence of the nascent
(load)

noche y la vaga melancolía de mi espíritu.
night and the vague melancholy of my spirit

Impulsado de un pensamiento religioso, espontáneo
Impulsed of a thought religious spontaneous
(Pushed)

e indefinible, eché maquinalmente pie a tierra,
and indefinite (I) threw automatically foot to earth

me descubrí, y comencé a buscar en el fondo
myself uncovered and started to search in the depth

de mi memoria una de aquellas oraciones que me
of my memory one of those prayers that me

enseñaron cuando niño; una de aquellas
(they) taught when (I was) kid one of those

oraciones que, cuando más tarde se escapan
prayers that when more late itself (they) escape

involuntarias de nuestros labios, parece que
involuntarily from our lips seem that

aligeran el pecho oprimido, y semejantes a las
(they) lighten the breast oppressed and similar to the

lágrimas, alivian el dolor, que también toma estas
tears lightened the pain that also took these

formas para evaporarse.
forms for to evaporate itself

Ya había comenzado a murmurarla, cuando
Already (I had) started to murmur it when

de improviso sentí que me sacudían con violencia
of unexpected (I) felt that me (they) shook with violence
unexpectedly

por los hombros.
by the shoulders

Volví la cara: un hombre estaba al lado mío.
(I) turned the face a man was at the side my
at my side

Era uno de nuestros guías, natural del país,
(It) was one of our guides native of the country

el cual, con una indescriptible expresión de terror
the which with an indescribable expression of terror

pintada en el rostro, pugnaba por arrastrarme
painted on the face fought for to drag me

consigo y cubrir mi cabeza con el fieltro que
with him and cover my face with the felt that

aún tenía en mis manos.
still (I) had in my hands

Mi primera mirada, mitad de asombro, mitad de
My first look half of surprise half of

cólera, equivalía a una interrogación enérgica,
anger   equaled   to   an   interrogation   energetic

aunque muda.
although   silent

El pobre hombre, sin cejar en su empeño de
The   poor   man   without to cease in his endeavor of

alejarme de aquel sitio, contestó a ella con
to distance me of   that   site   answered to   that   with
{my look}

estas palabras, que entonces no pude
these   words   that   then   not   (I) could

comprender, pero en las que había un acento de
comprehend but in those that had an accent of

verdad que me sobrecogió: - ¡Por la memoria de
truth that me over-caught   For the memory of
(startled)

su madre! ¡Por lo más sagrado que tenga en
your mother For the most sacred that (you) have in

el mundo, señorito, cúbrase usted la cabeza,
the world little sir cover yourself you the head

y aléjese más que de prisa de esta cruz!
and distance yourself more than of haste from this cross

¡Tan desesperado está usted, que no bastándole la
So desperate are you that not enough to you the

ayuda de Dios, recurre a la del demonio!
help of God (you) recur to that of the devil

Yo permanecí un rato mirándole en silencio.
I remained a while looking at him in silence

Francamente, creí que estaba loco, pero él
Frankly (I) believed that (he) was mad but he

prosiguió con igual vehemencia:
continued with equal vehemence

- Usted busca la frontera; pues bien, si delante
You search the border then well if in front

de esa cruz le pide usted al cielo que le
of that cross him ask you to the heaven that him

preste ayuda, las cumbres de los montes vecinos
gives (you) help the summits of the mountains close

se levantarán en una sola noche hasta las
themselves rose in a single night towards the

estrellas invisibles, sólo porque no encontremos la
stars invisible only because not (we) encountered the

raya en toda nuestra vida.
ray in all our life

Yo no pude menos de sonreír.
I not could less of smile
(than)

- ¿Se burla usted?... ¿cree acaso que esa es
Yourself joke you (you) believe maybe that that is
Are you kidding me

una cruz santa como la del porche de nuestra
a cross saintly like that of the porch of our

iglesia?...
church

- ¿Quién lo duda?
Who it doubts

- Pues se engaña usted de medio a medio,
Then yourself deceive you of half to half
you deceive yourself

porque esa cruz, salvo lo que tiene de Dios,
because that cross except that it belongs of God

está maldita... esa cruz pertenece a un espíritu
is cursed that cross belongs to a spirit

maligno, y por eso la llaman "La cruz del
malign and for that it (they) call The cross of the
(evil)

diablo".
devil

- ¡La cruz del diablo! - repetí cediendo a sus
The cross of the devil (I) repeated giving in to his

instancias, sin darme cuenta a mí mismo
petitions without to give myself count to me self

del involuntario temor que comenzó a
of the involuntary fear that started to

apoderarse de mi espíritu, y que me rechazaba
empower itself of my spirit and that me repulsed

como una fuerza desconocida de aquel lugar; -
like a force unknown from that place

¡la cruz del diablo! - ¡Nunca ha herido mi
the cross of the devil Never has wounded my

imaginación una amalgama más disparatada de dos
imagination an amalgam more disparate of two

ideas tan absolutamente enemigas!... - ¡Una
ideas so absolutely hostile (to each other) A

cruz... y del diablo!!! ¡Vaya, vaya! Fuerza será
cross and of the devil Go go Maybe (it) will be

que en llegando a la población me expliques este
that in arriving at the village me explains this

monstruoso absurdo.
monstrous absurdism

Durante este corto diálogo, nuestros camaradas,
During this short dialogue our comrades
(companions)

que habían picado sus cabalgaduras, se nos
that had spurred their mounts themselves (to) us

reunieron al pie de la cruz; yo les expliqué
reunited at the foot of the cross I them explained

en breves palabras lo que acababa de suceder;
in short words that what finished of to happen

monté nuevamente en mi rocín, y las
(I) mounted newly on my nag and the
(again)

campanas de la parroquia llamaban lentamente a
bells of the parish called slowly to

la oración, cuando nos apeamos en lo más
the prayer when we footed in the most
(dismounted)

escondido y lóbrego de los paradores de Bellver.
hidden and gloomy of the hostels of Bellver

LA CRUZ DEL DIABLO - II

LA CRUZ DEL DIABLO
The   Cross   Of The   Devil

II
2

Las   llamas   rojas   y   azules   se   enroscaban
The   flames   red   and   blue   themselves   coiled

chisporroteando a lo largo del grueso tronco de
sparkling   at the length of the   thick   trunk   of
              along the

encina que ardía en el ancho hogar; nuestras
holm oak   that   burned   on   the   broad   hearth   our

sombras,   que   se   proyectaban   temblando
shadows   that   themselves   projected   trembling

sobre   los   ennegrecidos   muros,   se
on   the   blackened   walls   themselves

empequeñecían o tomaban formas gigantescas,
made small or took forms gigantic

según la hoguera despedía resplandores más o
according to the fireplace dispatched resplendence more or
(as)

menos brillantes; el vaso de saúco, ora vacío,
less shining the cup of (the) elder now empty

ora lleno y no de agua, como cangilón de
now full and not of water like (the) bucket of

noria, había dado tres veces la vuelta en
(a) treadmill had given three times the turn in

derredor del círculo que formábamos junto al
around of the circle that (we) formed together at the

fuego, y todos esperaban con impaciencia la
fire and all awaited with impatience the

historia de "La cruz del diablo", que a guisa de
story of The cross of the devil that at guise of

postres de la frugal cena que acabábamos de
desserts of the frugal dinner that (we) finished -of-

consumir,   se   nos   había   prometido,   cuando
to consume   itself us   had   promised   when
                              (was)

nuestro   guía   tosió   por   dos   veces,   se   echó
our   guide coughed -for- two   times   himself threw

al   coleto   un   último   trago   de   vino,
to the   skin dress   a   last   gulp   of   wine

limpióse   con   el   revés   de   la   mano   la   boca,
cleaned -himself- with the back   of   the hand   the mouth
                                                            his

y   comenzó   de   este   modo:
and started   of   this   manner
                   (in)

- Hace   mucho   tiempo,   mucho   tiempo,   yo   no   sé
  Makes   much   time   much   time   I   not know
     A long time ago   a long time

cuánto,   pero   los   moros   ocupaban   aún   la   mayor
how much but   the   Moors   occupied   still the mayor
                                                      (biggest)

parte   de   España,   se   llamaban   condes
part   of   Spain   themselves   called   counts

nuestros   reyes,   y   las   villas   y   aldeas
our   kings   and the   small towns and villages

pertenecían en feudo a ciertos señores, que a su
belonged in feudal to certain lords that at their

vez prestaban homenaje a otros más poderosos,
time loaned hommage to other more powerful (ones)
(turn) (gave)

cuando acaeció lo que voy a referir a ustedes.
when happened it that (I) go to refer to you
(relate)

Concluida esta breve introducción histórica, el
Concluded this short introduction historical the

héroe de la fiesta guardó silencio durante algunos
hero of the feast guarded silence during some
(kept)

segundos como para coordinar sus recuerdos, y
seconds as for to coordinate his memories and

prosiguió así:
continued thus

- Pues es el caso, que en aquel tiempo remoto,
Then (it) is the case that in that time remote

esta villa y algunas otras formaban parte
this small town and some others formed part

del   patrimonio de un noble barón, cuyo castillo
of the patrimony   of a   noble baron whose castle

señorial se   levantó por muchos siglos   sobre la
lordly   itself arose   for many   centuries on   the

cresta de un peñasco que   baña   el   Segre,
crest   of a   crag   that bathed   the   (river) Segre
                               (was washed by)

del   cual   toma   su   nombre.
of the which (it) took its   name

Aún   testifican la   verdad de mi relación algunas
Still testify   the truth   of my story   some

informes ruinas que, cubiertas de   jaramago   y
formless ruins   that covered   of   wall-rocket   and
                                   (with){plant: diplotaxis}

musgo,   se   alcanzan   a ver   sobre su   cumbre
moss   themselves achieve   to see on   its summit
                     and can just be seen

desde el   camino que   conduce a   este pueblo.
from   the road   that leads   to this village

No   sé   si, por ventura o   desgracia, quiso   la
Not   (I) know if   by   chance   or disgrace   wanted the

suerte que este señor, a quien por crueldad
fortune that this lord -at- whom for cruelty

detestaban sus vasallos, y por sus malas
detested his vassals and for whose bad

cualidades ni el rey admitía en la corte, ni
qualities neither the king admitted in the court nor

sus vecinos en el hogar, se aburriese de vivir
his neighbors in the home himself got bored of to live

solo con su mal humor y sus ballesteros en lo
alone with his bad mood and his crossbowmen in the

alto de la roca en que sus antepasados colgaron
height of the rock on that his ancestors hung
(which)

su nido de piedra.
their nest of stone

Devanábase noche y día los sesos en busca de
(He) Rolled himself night and day the brains in search of

alguna distracción propia de su carácter, lo cual
some distraction proper of his character the which
(suited) (to)

era   bastante   difícil,   después   de   haberse
was   enough   difficult   after   of   to have himself

cansado como   ya   lo estaba, de mover guerra a
tired   as   already it was   of moving war   to

sus vecinos, apalear a sus servidores y   ahorcar
his neighbors   impale to his   servants   and hang

a sus súbditos.
to his subjects

En esta ocasión cuentan las crónicas que se le
On this occasion   tell   the chronicles that itself him

ocurrió, aunque   sin   ejemplar, una idea feliz.
occurred although without example   an idea happy
                                                good idea

Sabiendo que los cristianos de otras poderosas
Knowing   that the Christians of other   powerful

naciones   se   aprestaban a partir juntos en
nations   themselves readied   to part   together in

una formidable armada a un país maravilloso para
a   formidable   army   to a land wondrous   for

conquistar el sepulcro de Nuestro Señor
to conquer the sepulcher of Our Lord

Jesucristo, que los moros tenían en su poder,
Jesus Christ that the Moors had in their power

se determinó a marchar en su seguimiento.
himself determined to march in their following
(decided) (trail)

Si realizó esta idea con objeto de purgar sus
Himself realized this idea with object of to purge his

culpas, que no eran pocas, derramando su sangre
guilts that not were few spilling his blood

en tan justa empresa, o con el de
in such just enterprise or with that of

trasplantarse a un punto donde sus malas
to transplant himself to a point here his bad
(place)

mañas no se conociesen, se ignora;
trickeries not themselves knew itself ignores
{manners} were known (the reason) is not known

pero la verdad del caso es que, con gran
but the truth of the case is that with great

contentamiento de grandes y chicos, de vasallos
contentment   of   adults and kids of   vassals
(satisfaction)

y de iguales, allegó cuánto dinero pudo,
and of equals arrived how much money (as he) could
(gathered)

redimió a sus pueblos del señorío, mediante
redeemed -to- his villages of the lordship by means of
(ransomed) (fiefdom) (acquiring)

una gruesa cantidad, y no conservando de
a gross quantity and not conserving of
(large)

propiedad suya más que el peñón del Segre y
property his more than the crag of the Segre and

las cuatro torres del castillo, herencia de sus
the four towers of the castle inheritance of his

padres, desapareció de la noche a la mañana.
fathers disappeared of the night to the morning
(in) (by)

La comarca entera respiró en libertad durante
The region entire breathed in freedom during
entire region

algún tiempo, como si despertara de una
some time as if (it) woke up from a

pesadilla.
nightmare

Ya		no	colgaban	de	los	árboles	de	sus	sotos,
Already		not	hung	from	the	trees	of	its	thickets

en	vez	de	frutas,	racimos	de	hombres:	las
in	time	of	fruits	clusters	of	men	the
instead							

muchachas	del	pueblo	no	temían	al	salir	con
girls	of the	village	not	feared	at the	exit	with

su	cántaro	en	la	cabeza	a	tomar	agua	de	la
their	pitcher	on	the	head	to	get	water	from	the

fuente	del	camino,	ni	los	pastores	llevaban	sus
fountain	of the	road	nor	the	shepherds	brought	their
	(at the)						

rebaños	al	Segre	por	sendas	impracticables	y
flocks	to the	Segre	by	paths	impractical	and

ocultas,	temblando	encontrar	a	cada	revuelta	de
hidden	trembling	to encounter	at	each	turn	of

la	trocha	a	los	ballesteros	de	su	muy
the	narrow road	-to-	the	crossbowmen	of	their	much

amado señor.
beloved   lord
{ironical}

Así   transcurrió   el   espacio   de   tres   años;   la
Thus   transpired   the   space   of   three   years   the

historia   del   "mal   caballero",   que   sólo   por   este
history   of the   bad   knight   that   only   by   this

nombre   se   le   conocía,   comenzaba   a
name   himself   to him   knew   started   to
                           (was known)

pertenecer   al   exclusivo   dominio   de   las   viejas,
pertain   to the   exclusive   domain   of   the   old ones

que   en   las   eternas   veladas   del   invierno   las
that   on   the   eternal   wakes   of the   winter   them

relataban   con   voz   hueca   y   temerosa   a   los
told   with   voice   hollow   and   fearful   to   the

asombrados   chicos;   las   madres   asustaban   a   los
amazed   boys   the   mothers   frightened   -to-   the

pequeñuelos incorregibles   o   llorones   diciéndoles:
small ones   incorrigible   or   weepers   telling them
    incorrigible small ones   (crybabies)

"¡que viene el señor del Segre!" cuando he
that comes the lord of the Segre when (I) have

aquí que no sé si un día o una noche, si caído
here that not knows if a day or a night if fallen

del cielo o abortado de los profundos, el
from the sky or aborted of the depths the
(kicked out)

temido señor apareció efectivamente, y como
feared lord appeared effectively and as

suele decirse, en carne y hueso, en mitad
usually to say oneself in flesh and bone in (the) middle

de sus antiguos vasallos.
of his old vassals

Renuncio a describir el efecto de esta agradable
Renounce to describe the effect of this pleasant
(I abandon) {ironical}

sorpresa. Ustedes se lo podrán figurar mejor
surprise You yourself it will be able to figure better

que yo pintarlo, sólo con decirles que tornaba
than I paint it only with to say you that (he) returned
(can describe it)

reclamando   sus   vendidos   derechos,   que   si   malo
demanding   his   sold   rights   that   if   bad

se   fue,   peor   volvió,   y   si   pobre   y   sin
-himself- (he) was   worse   returned   and   if   poor   and   without
he was before

crédito   se   encontraba   antes   de   partir   a   la
credit   himself   encountered   before   of   to leave   to   the

guerra,   ya   no   podía   contar   con   más   recursos
war   already   not   could   count   with   more   resources

que   su   despreocupación,   su   lanza   y   una   media
than   his   unconcern   his   lance   and   a   half
                (disregard for all)

docena   de   aventureros   tan   desalmados   y   perdidos
dozen   of   adventurers   so   soulless   and   lost

como   su   jefe.
as   their   chief

Como   era   natural,   los   pueblos   se   resistieron
As   was   natural   the   villages   themselves   resisted

a   pagar   tributes,   que   a   tanta   costa   habían
to   pay   tributes   that   at   so much   cost   (they) had

redimido; **pero** **el** **señor** **puso** **fuego** **a** **sus**
redeemed but the lord set fire to their
(paid off)

heredades, **a** **sus** **alquerías** **y** **a** **sus** **mieses.**
properties to their farmsteads and to their wheats
(fields)

Entonces **apelaron** **a** **la** **justicia** **del** **rey;** **pero** **el**
Then (they) called at the justice of the king but the

señor **se** **burló** **de** **las** **cartas-leyes** **de** **los**
lord himself made fun of the letter-laws of the

Condes **soberanos;** **las** **clavó** **en** **el** **postigo** **de**
counts sovereign them (he) nailed in the posterns of
sovereign counts

sus **torres,** **y** **colgó** **a** **los** **farsantes** **de** **una**
his towers and hung -to- the bluffers from a

encina.
holm oak

Exasperados, **y** **no** **encontrando** **otra** **vía** **de**
Exasperated and not encountering (an) other way of
(finding)

salvación, **por** **último,** **se** **pusieron** **de**
salvation for last themselves set of
(at)

acuerdo entre sí, se encomendaron a
agreement between each other themselves recommended to
(entrusted)

la Divina Providencia y tomaron las armas; pero
the divine providence and took the arms but

el señor reunió a sus secuaces, llamó en su
the lord reunited to his minions called in his

ayuda al diablo, se encaramó a su roca y
help to the devil himself perched at his rock and

se preparó a la lucha. Ésta comenzó terrible
himself prepared to the battle This started terrible

y sangrienta. Se peleaba con todas armas, en
and bloody Oneself fought with all arms in

todos sitios y a todas horas, con la espada y
all sites and at all hours with the sword and

el fuego, en la montaña y en la llanura, en el
the fire on the mountain and on the plains in the

día y durante la noche.
day and during the night

Aquello no era pelear para vivir; era vivir para
That not was fighting to live (it) was living to

pelear.
fight

Al cabo triunfó la causa de la justicia. Oigan
At the end triumphed the cause of the justice Hear

ustedes cómo.
you how

Una noche obscura, muy obscura, en que no se
One night dark very dark in that not itself
A dark night

oía ni un rumor en la tierra ni brillaba un
heard neither a sound on the ground nor shone a

solo astro en el cielo, los señores de la
single star in the heaven the lords of the

fortaleza, engreídos por una reciente victoria,
fortress conceited by a recent victory

se repartían el botín, y ebrios con el
themselves divided the booty and drunken with the

vapor de los licores en mitad de la loca y
vapor of the liquors in (the) middle of the crazy and

estruendosa orgía, entonaban sacrílegos cantares en
roaring orgy intoned sacrilegious songs in

loor de su infernal patrono.
praise of their infernal patron

Como dejo dicho, nada se oía en derredor
As (I) let said nothing itself heard in around

del castillo, excepto el eco de las blasfemias,
of the castle except the echo of the blasphemies

que palpitaban, perdidas en el sombrío seno de
that pounded lost in the dark bossom of

la noche, como palpitan las almas de los
the night like throbbed the souls of the

condenados envueltas en los pliegues del huracán
condemned enveloped in the folds of the hurricane

de los infiernos.
of the infernos
      hell

Ya los descuidados centinelas habían fijado
Already the careless sentinels had fixed

algunas veces sus ojos en la villa que
some times their eyes in the small town that

reposaba silenciosa, y se habían dormido
reposed in silence and themselves had fallen asleep

sin temor a una sorpresa, apoyados en el
without fear to a surprise supported in the
(by)

grueso tronco de sus lanzas, cuando he aquí
thick trunk of their lances when (I) have here

que algunos aldeanos, resueltos a morir y
that some villagers decided to die and

protegidos por la sombra, comenzaron a escalar
protected by the darkness started to climb

el cubierto peñón del Segre, a cuya cima
the covered crag of the Segre at whose summit

tocaron a punto de la media noche.
(they) touched at point of the middle (of the) night
(they reached)

Una vez en la cima, lo que faltaba por hacer
One time on the summit that what lacked for to do

fue obra de poco tiempo: los centinelas salvaron
was work of little time the sentinels saved

de un solo salto el valladar que separa al
of a single jump the fence that separated -to- the

sueño de la muerte; el fuego aplicado con
sleep from -the- death the fire applied with

teas de resina al puente y al rastrillo, se
torches of pitch to the bridge and to the portculles itself

comunicó con la rapidez del relámpago a los
communicated with the speed of the lightning to the
(spread)

muros; y los escaladores, favorecidos por la
walls and the stairs favored by the

confusión y abriéndose paso entre las llamas,
confusion and opening itself pass between the flames

dieron fin con los habitantes de aquella guarida en
gave end with the inhabitants of that den in

un abrir y cerrar de ojos.
an opening and closing of eyes

Todos perecieron.
All perished

Cuando el cercano día comenzó a blanquear las
When the nearby day began to whiten the

altas copas de los enebros, humeaban aún los
high tops of the junipers smoked still the

calcinados escombros de las desplomadas torres,
calcined debris from the collapsed towers

y a través de sus anchas brechas, chispeando
and -at- through of its wide gaps sparkling

al herirla la luz y colgada de uno de los
at the wounding it the light and hanging from one of the

negros pilares de la sala del festín, era fácil
black pillars of the hall of the feast (it) was easy

divisar la armadura del temido jefe, cuyo
to perceive the armor of the feared chief whose

35

cadáver, cubierto de sangre y polvo, yacía
cadaver covered of blood and dust lay
(with)

entre los desgarrados tapices y las calientes
between the torn tapestries and the hot

cenizas, confundido con los de sus obscuros
ashes confused with those of his dark
(mixed)

compañeros.
companions

LA CRUZ DEL DIABLO - III

LA CRUZ DEL DIABLO
The Cross Of The Devil

III
3

El   tiempo   pasó;   comenzaron   los   zarzales   a
The   time   passed   started   the   brambles   to

rastrear por los desiertos patios, la hiedra a
trace   for   the   deserted   patios   the   ivy   to
crawl over

enredarse en los obscuros machones, y las
tangle itself in   the   dark   supports   and   the

campanillas azules a   mecerse   colgadas de las
little bells   blue   to sway themselves   hung   from the
bluebells

mismas   almenas. Los desiguales soplos de la
same   battlements The   unequal   breaths   of   the
(very)   (irregular)

brisa, el graznido de las aves nocturnas y el
breeze the squawk of the birds nocturnal and the

rumor de los reptiles, que se deslizaban
sound of the reptiles that themselves slithered

entre las altas hierbas, turbaban sólo
between the high grasses disturbed only

de vez en cuando el silencio de muerte de aquel
of time in when the silence of death of that
    now and then

lugar maldecido; los insepultos huesos de sus
place accursed the unburied bones of its

antiguos moradores blanqueaban al rayo de la
ancient residents whitened at the ray of the

luna, y aún podía verse el haz de armas del
moon and still could itself see the bundle of arms of the
    (armor)

señor del Segre, colgado del negro pilar de
lord of the Segre hung from the black pillar of

la sala del festín.
the hall of the feast

Nadie osaba tocarle; pero corrían mil
Nobody dared touch it but (there) ran (a) thousand

fábulas acerca de aquel objeto, causa incesante de
fables about of that object cause incessantly of
(myths)

hablillas y terrores para los que le miraban
talks and terrors for those that it watched

llamear durante el día, herido por la luz
burn during the day wounded by the light
{metaphorically} {metaphorically}

del sol, o creían percibir en las altas horas de
of the sun or believed to perceive in the high hours of
(late)

la noche el metálico son de sus piezas, que
the night the metallic sound of its pieces that

chocaban entre sí cuando las movía el
bumped between each other when them moved the

viento, con un gemido prolongado y triste.
wind with a groaning prolonged and sad

A pesar de todos los cuentos que a propósito de
At weight of all the stories that about -of-

la   armadura   se   fraguaron,   y   que   en   voz
the   armor   themselves   forged   and   that   in   voice
were forged

baja   se   repetían   unos   a   otros   los
low   themselves   repeated   ones   to   (the) others   the
were repeated

habitantes   de   los   alrededores,   no   pasaban   de
inhabitants   of   the   surroundings   not   passed   of

cuentos,   y   el   único   más   positivo   que   de   ello
tales   and   the   only   more   positive   that   of   them

resultó,   se   redujo   entonces   a   una   dosis   de
resulted   itself   reduced   then   to   a   doses   of

miedo   más   que   regular,   que   cada   uno   de   por   sí
fear   more   than   regular   that   each   one   of   for   itself

se   esforzaba   en   disimular   lo   posible,   haciendo,
itself   forced   in   hide   the   possible   making

como   decirse   suele,   de   tripas   corazón.
as   to say oneself   uses   of   insides   (a) heart

Si   de   aquí   no   hubiera   pasado   la   cosa,   nada   se
If   of   here   not   had   passed   the   thing   nothing   itself
(happened)

habría   perdido.   Pero   el   diablo,   que
would have   lost   But   the   devil   that
(would be)   (who)

a lo que parece   no   se   encontraba   satisfecho
to it that seems   not   himself encountered   satisfied
    as it seems   was

de su obra,   sin   duda, con el permiso de Dios
of his work without doubt With the permission of God

  y a fin de hacer purgar a la comarca algunas
and at end of to make purge to the region   some

culpas, volvió a tomar cartas en el asunto.
guilts returned to take cards in the matter

Desde este momento las fábulas, que hasta aquella
From this moment the fables that until that
                  (myths)

época no pasaron de un rumor vago y   sin
epoch not surpassed -of- a rumor vague and without
(time)

viso alguno de verosimilitud, comenzaron a tomar
gleam any of plausibility started to take
    any prove

consistencia y a hacerse de día en día
consistence and to make themselves from day in day

más   probables.
more   probable

En   efecto,   hacía   algunas   noches   que   todo   el
In   effect   had   some   nights   that   all   the
                    (there were)

pueblo   había   podido   observar   un   extraño
people   had   been able   to observe   a   strange

fenómeno.
phenomenon

Entre   las   sombras,   a   lo   lejos,   ya   subiendo
Between   the   shadows   at   the   distance   already   going up

las   retorcidas   cuestas   del   peñón   del   Segre,
the   twisted   slopes   of the   crag   of the   Segre

ya   vagando   entre   las   ruinas   del   castillo,
already   wandering   between   the   ruins   of the   castle

ya   cerniéndose   al   parecer   en   los   aires,   se
already   hovering itself   at the   to seem   in   the   airs   itself
                                  seemingly

veían   correr,   cruzarse,   esconderse   y   tornar   a
(they) saw   run   cross itself   hide itself   and   turn   to

aparecer para alejarse en distintas direcciones
appear for to go away itself in various directions

unas luces misteriosas y fantásticas cuya
some lights mysterious and fantasy-like which

procedencia nadie sabía explicar.
origin no one knew to explain
could explain

Esto se repitió por tres o cuatro noches durante
This itself repeated for three or four nights during

el intervalo de un mes; y los confusos aldeanos
the interval of a month and the confused villagers

esperaban inquietos el resultado de aquellos
awaited restless the result of those

conciliábulos, que ciertamente no se hizo
secret gatherings that certainly not itself made

aguardar mucho, cuando tres o cuatro alquerías
await much when three or four farmhouses

incendiadas, varias reses desaparecidas y los
burned various cattle disappeared and the

cadáveres de algunos caminantes despeñados en
corpses   of   some   travelers   knocked off   in

los precipicios, pusieron en alarma todo el
the   precipices   set   in   alarm   all   the

territorio en diez leguas a la redonda.
territory   in   ten   leagues   to the   circle
                                    around

Ya no quedó duda alguna. Una banda de
Already   not   remained   doubt   any   A   band   of

malhechores se albergaba en los subterráneos
malefactors   itself   harbored   in   the   undergrounds

del castillo.
of the   castle

Estos, que sólo se presentaban al principio
These   that   only   themselves   presented   at the   beginning

muy de tarde en tarde y en determinados puntos
very   of   late   in   late   and   in   certain   points

del bosque que, aún en el día, se dilata
of the   forest   that   still   in   the   day   itself   expanded

a lo largo de la ribera, concluyeron por ocupar
at the length of the river   concluded   by to occupy
   along

casi todos los desfiladeros de las montañas,
almost all the gaps of the mountains

emboscarse en los caminos, saquear los valles
ambush -themselves- on the roads sack the vallies
     (plunder)

y descender como un torrente a la llanura,
and descend like a torrent to the flat(s)

donde, a éste quiero, a éste no quiero, no
where to this (I) want to this not (I) want not

dejaban títere con cabeza.
left (a) puppet with (a) head

Los asesinatos se multiplicaban; las
The assassins themselves multiplied the

muchachas desaparecían, y los niños eran
girls disappeared and the children were

arrancados de las cunas a pesar de los lamentos
torn from the cradles at weight of the laments
     in spite of

de sus madres, para servirlos en diabólicos
of their mothers to serve them in diabolic

festines, en que, según la creencia general, los
feasts in that according to believe common the
common believe

vasos sagrados sustraídos de las profanadas
cups sacred subtracted from the desecrated
sacred cups (taken)

iglesias servían de copas.
churches served of glasses

El terror llego a apoderarse de los ánimos en
The terror arrived to overcome itself of the spirits in

un grado tal, que al toque de oraciones nadie
a degree such that at the strike of prayers no one
(time)

se aventuraba a salir de su casa, en la que
himself dared to exit from his house in it that
where

no siempre se creían seguros de los
not always themselves (they) believed secure from the
(even)

bandidos del peñón.
bandits of the crag

Mas ¿quiénes eran éstos? ¿De dónde habían
More who are these From where have (they)

venido? ¿Cuál era el nombre de su misterioso
come Which is the name of their mysterious

jefe? He aquí el enigma que todos querían
chief (I) Have here the enigma that all wanted

explicar y que nadie podía resolver hasta
to explain and that no one could resolve until

entonces, aunque se observase desde luego que
then although itself was observed from after that
of course

la armadura del señor feudal había desaparecido
the armor of the lord feudal had disappeared
feudal lord

del sitio que antes ocupara, y posteriormente
from the site that before (it) occupied and after

varios labradores hubiesen afirmado que el capitán
various workers had affirmed that the captain

de aquella desalmada gavilla marchaba a su frente,
of that soulless bunch marched at its front

cubierto con una, que de no ser la misma, se le
covered with one that of not be the same itself it
maybe not

asemejaba en un todo.
looked like in an all
totally looked like

Cuanto queda repetido, si se le despoja de
How much remained repeated if itself to it strips away of

esa parte de fantasía con que el miedo abulta y
that part of fantasy with that the fear bulges and
(adds)

completa sus creaciones favoritas, nada tiene en
completes ones creations favorite nothing had in
favorite creations

sí de sobrenatural y extraño. ¿Qué cosa más
it of supernatural and strange What case more

corriente en unos bandidos que las ferocidades
running in some bandits than the ferocities
(normal)

con que estos se distinguían, ni más natural
with that these themselves distinguished nor more natural

que el apoderarse su jefe de las
than the empower themselves their chief of the
(acquiring)

abandonadas armas del señor del Segre?
abandoned arms of the lord of the Segre
(armor)

Sin embargo, algunas revelaciones hechas antes
Without embargo some revelations made before
Nevertheless

de morir por uno de sus secuaces, prisionero en
of to die by one of his minions (made) prisoner in

las últimas refriegas, acabaron de colmar la
the last skirmishes finished of to top up the

miedo, preocupando el ánimo de los más
fear occupying the spirit of the most

incrédulos. Poco más o menos, el contenido de
unbelieving (A) Bit more or less the content of

su confesión fue éste: - Yo, dijo, pertenezco a
his confession was this I (I) say belong to

una noble familia. Los extravíos de mi juventud,
a noble family The deviations of my youth

mis locas prodigalidades y mis crímenes por
my crazy prodigalities and my crimes for
(at)

49

último atrajeron sobre mi cabeza la cólera de mis
last   attracted   on   my   head   the   anger   of   my

deudos y la maldición de mi padre, que me
debtors   and   the   curse   of   my   father   that   me

desheredó al expirar. Hallándome solo y sin
disinherited   at the   to expire   Finding myself   alone   and   without
    at his death

recursos de ninguna especie, el diablo sin duda
resources   of   none   kind   the   devil   without   doubt
    (any)

debió sugerirme la idea de reunir algunos
must   suggest to me   the   idea   of   to reunite   some

jóvenes que se encontraban en una situación
youths   that   themselves   encountered   in   a   situation

idéntica a la mía, los cuales, seducidos con las
identical   to   the   mine   the   which   seduced   with   the

promesas de un porvenir de disipación, libertad,
promises   of   a   future   of   dissipation   liberty
    (debauchery)

y abundancia, no vacilaron un instante en
and   abundance   not   (they) hesitated   an   instant   in

suscribir   a   mis   designios.
to subscribe to   my   designs
                         (plan)

Éstos   se   reducían   a   formar   una   banda   de
These   themselves   reduced   to   form   a   band   of
                  set

jóvenes   de   buen   humor,   despreocupados   y   poco
youths   of   good   mood   unworried   and   little
                                                              (not)

temerosos   del   peligro,   que   desde   allí   en   adelante
afraid   of the   danger   that   from   then   on   forward

vivirían   alegremente   del   producto   de   su   valor
(they) lived   happily   of the   product   of   their   valor

y   a   costa   del   país,   hasta   tanto   que   Dios
and   at (the) cost of the   country   until   so much   that   God

se   sirviera   disponer   de   cada   uno   de   ellos
himself   served   to dispose   of   each   one   of   them

conforme   a   su   voluntad,   según   hoy   a   mí
conform   to   his   will   according to   today   to   myself
                                  (which)

me   sucede.
me   (it) succeeds
      (it) happens

Con este objeto señalamos esta comarca para
With this object (we) signed this region to

teatro de nuestras expediciones futuras, y
theater of our expeditions future and
future expeditions

escogimos como punto el más a propósito para
chose as point the most to aim for
adequate

nuestras reuniones el abandonado castillo del
our reunions the abandoned castle of the

Segre, lugar seguro, no tanto por su posición
Segre place secure not so much for its position

fuerte y ventajosa, como por hallarse
strong and advantageous as for to find themselves

defendido contra el vulgo por las
defended against the vulgar by the
(common people)

supersticiones y el miedo.
superstitions and the fear

Congregados una noche bajo sus ruinosas arcadas,
Gathered one night under its ruined arcades

alrededor de una hoguera que iluminaba con su
around -of- a bonfire that lit with its

rojizo resplandor las desiertas galerías, trabóse
reddish resplendent the deserted galleries locked itself
(shine) (was carried on)

una acalorada disputa sobre cuál de nosotros
a heated dispute about whom of us

había de ser elegido jefe.
had of to be chosen chief

Cada uno alegó sus méritos; yo expuse mis
Each one alleged his merits I exposed my
(summed up) (laid out)

derechos: ya los unos murmuraban entre
rights already the ones murmured between
some

sí con ojeadas amenazadoras; ya los otros
each other with glances threatening already the others
some others

con voces descompuestas por la embriaguez
with voices decomposed by the drunkenness
(slurring)

habían puesto la mano sobre el pomo de sus
had put the hand on the pommel of their

puñales para dirimir la cuestión, cuando
daggers for to settle the question when

de repente oímos un extraño crujir de armas,
of sudden (we) heard a strange creaking of arms
suddenly (armor)

acompañado de pisadas huecas y sonantes, que
accompanied of steps hollow and sounding that
(by) (ringing)

de cada vez se hacían más distintas.
-of- each time themselves made more distinct

Todos arrojamos a nuestro alrededor una inquieta
All throw at our surroundings a worried
We all throw

mirada de desconfianza; nos pusimos de pie
look of distrust we put ourselves of feet
(on our)

y desnudamos nuestros aceros, determinados a
and bare our irons determined to
(weapons)

vender caras las vidas; pero no pudimos
sell expensive the lives but not (we) can

por menos de permanecer inmóviles al ver
for least of remain immobile at the to see
more than at seeing

adelantarse   con   paso   firme   e   igual   un   hombre
approaching itself   with   step   firm   and   equal   a   man
(regular)

de elevada estatura, completamente armado de la
of   risen   standing   completely   armed   from   the
    tall stature

cabeza   al   pie   y   cubierto   el   rostro   con   la
head   to the   foot   and   covered   the   face   with   the

visera   del   casco,   el   cual,   desnudando   su
visor   of the   helmet   the   which   undressing   his
    (unsheathing)

montante,   que   dos   hombres   podrían   apenas
support-bar   that   two   men   could   hardly
(two handed sword)

manejar,   y   poniéndole   sobre   uno   de   los
manage   and   putting it   on   one   of   the

carcomidos   fragmentos   de   las   rotas   arcadas,
rotten   fragments   of   the   broken   arcades

exclamó   con   una   voz   hueca   y   profunda,
exclaimed   with   a   voice   hollow   and   deep

semejante   al   rumor   de   una   caída   de   aguas
similar   to the   sound   of   a   fall   of   waters

subterráneas:
subterranean
(underground)

- Si   alguno   de   vosotros   se   atreve   a   ser   el
  If   anyone   of   you   himself   dares   to   be   the

primero,   mientras   yo   habite   en   el   castillo   del
first   while   I   live   in   the   castle   of the

Segre,   que   tome   esa   espada,   signo   del   poder.
Segre   than   take   this   sword   sign   of the   power

Todos   guardamos   silencio,   hasta   que,   transcurrido
All   (we) guarded   silence   until   that   (having) elapsed
        We all kept silent

el   primer   momento   de   estupor,   le   proclamamos
the   first   moment   of   daze   him   (we) proclaimed

a   grandes   voces   nuestro   capitán,   ofreciéndole   una
at   great   voices   our   captain   offering him   a
        (loud)

copa   de   nuestro   vino,   la   cual   rehusó   por   señas,
cup   of   our   wine   the   which   (he) refused   by   signs

acaso   por   no   descubrirse   la   faz,   que   en   vano
maybe   for   not   to uncover himself   the   face   that   in   vain

procuramos distinguir a través de las rejillas de
(we) tried to distinguish at through of the bars of
between

hierro que la ocultaban a nuestros ojos.
iron that it hid at our eyes
(for)

No obstante, aquella noche pronunciamos el más
Not hindering that night (we) pronounced the most
Nevertheless (we took)

formidable de los juramentos, y a la siguiente
formidable of -the- swears and at the next
(vows)

dieron principio nuestras nocturnas correrías. En
(we) gave beginning our nightly runnings In
(raids)

ellas nuestro misterioso jefe marchaba siempre
them our mysterious chief marched always

delante de todos. Ni el fuego le ataja, ni los
in front of all Neither the fire him tackles nor the
(cut)

peligros le intimidan, ni las lágrimas le
dangers him intimidated nor the tears him

conmueven: Nunca despliega sus labios; pero
moved Never (he) unfolded his lips but
(he opened)

cuando la sangre humea en nuestras manos, como
when the blood fumed in our hands as

cuando los templos se derrumban
when the temples -themselves- collapsed
(churches)

calcinados por las llamas: cuando las mujeres
calcinated by the flames when the women
(burned)

huyen espantadas entre las ruinas, y los niños
fled frightened between the ruins and the children

arrojan gritos de dolor, y los ancianos perecen a
uttered shouts of pain and the old ones died at

nuestros golpes, contesta con una carcajada de
our blows (he) answered with a loud laughter of

feroz alegría a los gemidos, a las imprecaciones
ferocity happy at the groans at the imprecations
(curses)

y a los lamentos.
and at the laments

Jamás se desnuda de sus armas ni abate
Never itself undressed of his arms nor brought down
(armor)

la visera de su casco después de la victoria, ni
the visor of his helmet after of the victory nor

participa del festín, ni se entrega al
participated of the feast nor himself gave over to the
(in the)

sueño. Las espadas que le hieren se
sleep The swords that him wounded themselves

hunden entre las piezas de su armadura, y
sunk between the pieces of his armor and

ni le causan la muerte, ni se retiran
neither him caused the death nor themselves pulled back

teñidas en sangre; el fuego enrojece su espaldar
dyed in blood the fire reddened his back

y su cota, y aún prosigue impávido entre
and his side and still (he) continued undaunted between

las llamas, buscando nuevas víctimas; desprecia
the flames searching new victims despised
(looked down on)

el oro, aborrece la hermosura, y no le
the gold was bored by -the- beauty and not him

inquieta   la   ambición.
worried   the   ambition

Entre   nosotros,   unos   le   creen   un   extravagante;
Between   us   some   him   believed   an   extravagant

otros   un   noble   arruinado,   que   por   un   resto   de
others   a   noble   ruined   that   for   a   rest   of
                       ruined noble   (remainder)

pudor   se   tapa   la   cara;   y   no   falta   quien
modesty   himself   covered   the   face   and   not   lacked   who

se   encuentra   convencido   de   que   es   el   mismo
himself   encountered   convinced   of   that   (it) is   the   same
              was

diablo   en   persona.
devil   in   person

El   autor   de   esas   revelaciones   murió   con   la
The   author   of   those   revelations   died   with   the

sonrisa   de   la   mofa   en   los   labios   y   sin
smile   of   the   mockery   in   the   lips   and   without

arrepentirse   de   sus   culpas;   varios   de   sus   iguales
to repent himself   of   his   guilts   various   of   his   equals
                          (guilt)

le siguieron en diversas épocas al suplicio;
him followed in diverse epochs at the torture

pero el temible jefe, a quien continuamente
but the fearsome chief to whom continually

se unían nuevos prosélitos, no cesaba en sus
themselves united new proselytes not ceased in his
(disciples)

desastrosas empresas.
disastrous undertakings
(destructive)

Los infelices habitantes de la comarca, cada vez
The unfortunate inhabitants of the region each time

más aburridos y desesperados, no acertaban
more weary and desperate not ascertained

ya con la determinación que debería tomarse
already with the determination that should oneself take

para concluir de un todo con aquel orden de
for to conclude of an all with that order of
once and for all

cosas, cada día más insoportable y triste.
things each day more unsupportable and sad

Inmediato a la villa, y oculto en el fondo de
Immediately to the village and hidden in the depth of
(Next)

un espeso bosque, vivía a esta sazón, en una
a thick forest lived at this season in a
(time)

pequeña ermita dedicada a San Bartolomé un
small hermitage dedicated to Saint Bartholomew a

santo hombre, de costumbres piadosas y
saintly man of habits pious and

ejemplares, a quien el pueblo tuvo siempre en
exemplary to whom the village had always in

olor de santidad, merced a sus saludables consejos
smell of saintliness thanks to his healthy advices

y acertadas predicciones.
and correct predictions

Este venerable ermitaño, a cuya prudencia y
This venerable hermit to whose prudence and

proverbial sabiduría encomendaron los vecinos de
proverbial wisdom commended the neighbors of
(entrusted)

Bellver la resolución de este difícil problema,
Bellver the resolution of this difficult problem

después de implorar la misericordia divina por
after of to implore the mercy divine for

medio de su santo Patrono, que, como ustedes
medium of his saint Patron that as you

no ignoran, conoce al diablo muy de cerca,
not ignore knows -to- the devil much of close
know

y en más de una ocasión le ha
and in more of one occasion him has
(than)

atado bien corto, les aconsejó que se
tied him short them advised that themselves
controlled him

emboscasen durante la noche al pie del
(they) ambush during the night at the foot of the

pedregoso camino que sube serpenteando por la
stony road that goes up snaking by the

roca, en cuya cima se encontraba el castillo,
rock in whose top itself encountered the castle

63

encargándoles al mismo tiempo que ya allí,
charging them at the same time that already there
(ordering them)

no hiciesen uso de otras armas para aprehenderlo
not (they) make use of other arms for to apprehend him

que de una maravillosa oración que les hizo
than of a wondrous prayer that them made

aprender de memoria, y con la cual aseguraban
learn of memory and with the which (they) assured

las crónicas que San Bartolomé había hecho al
the chronicles that Saint Bartholomew had made to the
(of the)

diablo su prisionero.'
devil his prisoner

Púsose en planta el proyecto, y su resultado
Set on floor the project and whose result
in motion

excedió a cuantas esperanzas se habían
exceeded to how much hopes themselves (they) had

concebido; pues aún no iluminaba el sol del otro
conceived then still not lit the sun of the other

día la alta torre de Bellver, cuando sus habitantes,
day the old tower of Bellver when its inhabitants

reunidos en grupos en la plaza Mayor, se
reunited in groups on the square mayor themselves

contaban unos a otros con aire de misterio,
recounted ones to (the) others with air of mystery

cómo aquella noche fuertemente atado de pies y
how that night strongly tied of feet and

manos y a lomos de una poderosa mula, había
hand and at (the) back of a powerful mule had

entrado en la población el famoso capitán de los
entered in the village the famous captain of the

bandidos del Segre.
bandits of the Segre

De qué arte se valieron los acometedores de
Of what art themselves availed the undertakers of

esta empresa para llevarla a término, ni nadie
this enterprise to take it at end neither no one

se   lo   acertaba   a   explicar,   ni   ellos   mismos
himself it   ascertained to   explain   nor   they   themselves

podían decirlo; pero el hecho era que, gracias a
could   tell it   but   the case   was that   thanks   to

la   oración   del   santo   o   al   valor   de   sus
the   prayer   of the saint   or   to the valor   of   its

devotos, la   cosa   había sucedido   tal   como   se
devotees   the thing   had   succeeded such   as   itself

refería.
referred

LA CRUZ DEL DIABLO - IV

LA CRUZ DEL DIABLO
The Cross Of The Devil

IV

Apenas la novedad comenzó a extenderse de
Hardly the novelty started to extend itself from
(spread)

boca en boca y de casa en casa, la multitud
mouth in mouth and from house in house the multitude
(to) (to)

se lanzó a las calles con ruidosa algazara, y
itself launched at the streets with noisy uproar and

corrió a reunirse a las puertas de la
ran to reunite themselves at the doors of the
(gather)

prisión. La campana de la parroquia llamó a
prison The bell from the parish called to

concejo, y los vecinos más respetables se
council and the neighbors most respectable themselves

juntaron en capítulo, y todos aguardaban ansiosos
joined in chapter and all awaited anxiously
(front)

la hora en que el reo había de comparecer
the hour in that the culprit had -of- to appear

ante sus improvisados jueces.
before his improvised judges

Éstos, que se encontraban autorizados por
These that themselves found authorized by

los condes de Urgel para
the counts of Urgel to

administrarse por sí mismos pronta y
administer -themselves- for themselves self quick and
administer by themselves

severa justicia sobre aquellos malhechores,
severe justice over those malefactors

deliberaron un momento, pasado el cual,
deliberated a moment passed the which
after which

mandaron comparecer al delincuente a fin de
(they) ordered — to appear — -to- the — delinquent — to — end — of
for

notificarle su sentencia.
to notify him — (of) his — sentence

Como dejo dicho, así en la plaza Mayor, como
As — (I) left — said — thus — on — the — square — large — as

en las calles por donde el prisionero debía
on — the — streets — by — where — the — prisoner — must

atravesar para dirigirse al punto en que sus
traverse — to — direct himself — to the — point — in — that — his

jueces se encontraban, la impaciente
judges — themselves — encountered — the — impatient
were located

multitud hervía como un apiñado enjambre de
multitude — boiled — like — a — crowded — swarm — of

abejas. Especialmente en la puerta de la cárcel,
bees — Especially — in — the — door — of — the — jail

la conmoción popular tomaba cada vez mayores
the — commotion — of the people — took — each — time — bigger

proporciones, y ya los animados diálogos, los
proportions and already the animated dialogues the

sordos murmullos y los amenazadores gritos
muted murmurs and the threatening shouts

comenzaban a poner en cuidado a sus guardas,
started to put in guard to its guards

cuando afortunadamente llego la orden de
when fortunately arrived the order of

sacar al reo.
to take out -to- the accused

Al aparecer éste bajo el macizo arco de la
At the to appear this (one) under the massive arch of the
When this one appeared

portada de su prisión, completamente vestido de
portal of his prison completely dressed of

todas armas y cubierto el rostro con la visera,
all arms and covered the face with the visor

un sordo y prolongado murmullo de admiración
a muted and prolonged murmuring of admiration

y   de   sorpresa   se   elevó   de   entre   las
and   of   surprise   themselves   raised   of   between   the

compactas   masas   del   pueblo,   que   se   abrían
compact   masses   of the   people   that   themselves   opened

con   dificultad   para   dejarle   paso.
with   difficulty   to   let him   pass

Todos   habían   reconocido   en   aquella   armadura   la
All   had   recognized   in   that   armor   that

del   señor   del   Segre;   aquella   armadura,   objeto   de
of the   lord   of the   Segre   that   armor   object   of

las   más   sombrías   tradiciones   mientras   se   la   vio
the   most   dismal   traditions   while   itself   it   saw
                                           it was seen

suspendida   de   los   arruinados   muros   de   la
suspended   from   the   ruined   walls   of   the

fortaleza   maldita.
fortress   cursed
cursed fortress

Las   armas   eran   aquellas,   no   cabía   duda   alguna;
The   arms   were   those   not   fit   doubt   any
        The armor was that

todos habían visto flotar el negro penacho de su
all had seen float the black plume of its

cimera en los combates, que en un tiempo
top in the combats that in one time
(battles)

trabaran contra su señor; todos le habían visto
waged against its lord all it had seen

agitarse al soplo de la brisa del crepúsculo,
move itself at the blow of the breeze of the dusk

a par de la hiedra del calcinado pilar en que
at pair of the ivy of the burned pilar in that
next to

quedaron colgadas a la muerte de su dueño. Mas
remained hung at the death of its owner More

¿quién podría ser el desconocido personaje que
who might see the unknown person that

entonces las llevaba? Pronto iba a saberse: al
then it wore Fast (it) went to know at the
it would be known

menos así se creía. Los sucesos dirán cómo
least thus itself believed The events will tell how
it was believed

esta esperanza quede frustrada, a la manera de
this hope remained frustrated at the manner of

otras muchas, y porqué de este solemne acto de
other many and because of this solemn act of

justicia, del que debía aguardarse el completo
justice of the that (one) must await itself the complete
    of which

esclarecimiento de la verdad, resultarán nuevas y
enlightenment of the truth (there) result new and

más inexplicables confusiones.
more unexplainable confusions

El misterioso bandido penetró al fin en la
The mysterious bandit penetrated at the end in(to) the

sala del concejo, y un silencio profundo sucedió
hall of the council and a silence profound followed
    complete silence

a los rumores que se elevaran de entre
to the rumors that themselves rose from between

los circunstantes, al oír resonar bajo las altas
the bystanders at the to hear resound under the high
    at hearing

bóvedas de aquel recinto el metálico son de sus
arches of that enclosure the metalic sound of his

acicates de oro. Uno de los que componían el
spurs of gold One of those that composed the
(who)

tribunal con voz lenta e insegura, le preguntó
tribunal with voice slow and insecure him asked

su nombre, y todos prestaron el oído con
his name and all lend the hearing with

ansiedad para no perder una sola palabra de su
anxiety for not to lose a sole word of his

respuesta; pero el guerrero se limitó a
response but the warrior himself limited to

encoger sus hombros ligeramente con un aire de
contract his shoulders slightly with an air of
shrug

desprecio e insulto, que no pudo menos
contempt and insult that not could less

de irritar a sus jueces, los que
of to irritate -to- his judges those that
than irritate

se miraron entre sí sorprendidos.
themselves looked at between each other surprised
        looked at each other

Tres veces volvió a repetirle la pregunta,
Three times (he) returned to repeat to him the question

y otras tantas obtuvo semejante o parecida
and other so much obtained (a) similar or alike

contestación.
answer

- ¡Que se levante la visera! ¡Que se
That himself (he) lifts the visor That himself

descubra! ¡Que se descubra! - comenzaron a
(he) uncovers That himself (he) uncovers started to

gritar los vecinos de la villa presentes al acto.
shout the neighbors of the village present at the scene

- ¡Que se descubra! ¡Veremos si se atreve
That himself (he) uncovers (We) will see if himself (he) dares

entonces a insultarnos con su desdén, como ahora
then to insult us with his disdain as now

lo   hace   protegido por   el   incógnito!
it   (he) does   protected   by   the   (being) incognito

\-   Descubríos,   \-   repitió   el   mismo   que
      Uncover yourself   repeated   the   same   that

anteriormente   le   dirigiera   la   palabra.
    before   him   directed   the   word

El   guerrero   permaneció   impasible.
The   warrior   remained   impassible

\-   Os   lo   mando   en   el   nombre   de   nuestra
    You   it   (I) order   in   the   name   of   our

autoridad.
  authority

La   misma   contestación.
The   same   answer

\- En   el   de los   condes   soberanos.'
   In   that   of   the   counts   sovereign
                  sovereign counts

Ni   por   ésas.
Not   for   those (either)

La indignación llegó a su colmo, hasta el punto
The indignation arrived at its summit until the point

de que uno de sus guardas, lanzándose sobre
-of- that one of his guards launching himself on

el reo, cuya pertinacia en callar bastaría
the accused whose pertinacity in keeping quiet was enough

para apurar la paciencia a un santo, le abrió
for drain the patience to a saint him opened
(of)

violentamente la visera. Un grito general de
violently the visor A shout general of

sorpresa se escapó del auditorio, que
surprise itself escaped from the audience that

permaneció por un instante herido de un
remained for an instant wounded of an
struck by

inconcebible estupor.
inconceivable stupor

La cosa no era para menos.
The thing not was for less (reaction)

El casco, cuya férrea visera se veía en parte
The helmet whose iron visor itself saw in part

levantada hasta la frente, en parte caída sobre la
lifted to the forehead in part fallen over the

brillante gola de acero, estaba vacío...
shining collar of iron was empty

completamente vacío.
completely empty

Cuando pasado ya el primer momento de
When passed already the first moment of
after

terror quisieron tocarle, la armadura se
terror (they) wanted to touch him the armor itself

estremeció ligeramente, y descomponiéndose en
shook slightly and decomposing itself in

piezas, cayó al suelo con un ruido sordo y
pieces fell to the ground with a noise dull and

extraño.
strange

La mayor parte de los espectadores, a la vista
The largest part of the spectators at the sight

del nuevo prodigio, abandonaron tumultuosamente
of the new wonder abandoned tumultuously
(noisily)

la habitación y salieron despavoridos a la plaza.
the room and exited terrified to the square

La nueva se divulgó con la rapidez del
The news itself spread with the speed of the

pensamiento entre la multitud, que aguardaba
thought between the crowd that awaited

impaciente el resultado del juicio; y fue tal
impatiently the result of the judgment and was such

la alarma, la revuelta y la vocería, que ya a
the panic the scramble and the clamor that already to

nadie cupo duda sobre lo que de pública voz
no one fit doubt over it that of public voice
by the public

se aseguraba, esto es, que el diablo, a la
itself assured that is that the devil at the
was affirmed

muerte del señor del Segre, había heredado los
death   of the   lord   of the   Segre   had   inherited   the

feudos de Bellver.
fiefs   of   Bellver

Al   fin   se   apaciguó   el   tumulto,   y   decidióse
At the   end   itself   pacified   the   uproar   and   decided itself
          calmed down   (it was decided)

volver   a   un   calabozo   la   maravillosa   armadura.
to return   to   a   (dungeon) cell   the   marvelous   armor

Ya   en él   despacháronse   cuatro   emisarios,   que
Already   in   it   dispatched themselves   four   emissaries   that

en   representación   de   la   atribulada   villa   hiciesen
in   representation   of   the   troubled   village   made

presente   el   caso   al   conde   de   Urgel   y   al
presence   the   case   to the   count   of   Urgel   and   to the

arzobispo,   los   que   no   tardaron   muchos   días   en
archbishop   those   that   not   delayed   much   days   in

tornar   con   la   resolución   de   estos   personajes,
to return   with   the   resolution   of   these   persons
          (decision)

resolución que, como suele decirse, era breve
resolution that as is used to say oneself was short
(decision)

y compendiosa.
and compendious

- Cuélguese, - les dijeron, - la armadura en la
Hang itself these said the armor on the

plaza Mayor de la villa; que, si el diablo la
square large of the village that if the devil it

ocupa, fuerza le será el abandonarla o
occupies maybe to him will he abandon it or

ahorcarse con ella.
hang himself with her

Encantados los habitantes de Bellver con tan
Enchanted the inhabitants of Bellver with such

ingeniosa solución, volvieron a reunirse en
ingenious solution returned to unite themselves in

concejo, mandaron levantar una altísima horca en
council ordered to erect a very high gallow(s) in

la plaza, y cuando ya la multitud ocupaba
the square and when already the multitude occupied

sus avenidas, se dirigieron a la cárcel por
its roads themselves directed to the jail for

la armadura, en corporación y con toda la
the armor in corporation and with all the
          all together

solemnidad que la importancia del caso requería.
solemnity that the importance of the case required

Cuando la respetable comitiva llego al macizo
When the respectable committee arrived at the massive

arco que daba entrada al edificio, un hombre
arch that gave entry to the building a man

pálido y descompuesto se arrojó al suelo
palid and decomposed himself threw at the ground
          (stressed)

en presencia de los aturdidos circunstantes,
in presence of the confused bystanders

exclamando con las lágrimas en los ojos:
exclaiming with the tears in the eyes

- Perdón, señores, perdón!
Pardon   lords   Pardon

- Perdón!; ¿Para quién? - dijeron algunos; - ¿para
Pardon   For   whom   said   some   for

el diablo, que habita dentro de la armadura del
the   devil   that   lived   inside   of   the   armor   of the

señor del Segre?
lord   of the   Segre

- Para mí, - prosiguió con voz trémula el
For   me   continued   with   voice   trembling   the

infeliz, en quien todos reconocieron al
infortunate   in   whom   all   recognized   -to- the

alcaide de las prisiones; - para mí... porque las
warden   of   the   prisons   for   me   because   the

armas... han desaparecido.
arms   have   disappeared
(armor)   (has)

Al oír estas palabras, el asombro se pintó
At the   to hear   these   words   the   surprise   itself   painted
   At hearing

en el rostro de cuantos se encontraban en
on the face of whomever themselves encountered in

el pórtico, que, mudos e inmóviles, hubieran
the portal that speechless and immobile had

permanecido en la posición en que se
remained in the position in that themselves

encontraban, Dios sabe hasta cuándo, si la
encountered God knows until when if the

siguiente relación del aterrado guardián no les
following tale of the terrified guardian not them

hubiera hecho agruparse en su alrededor para
had made group themselves in his vicinity for

escuchar con avidez:
to listen with avidity
(keenness)

- Perdonadme, señores, - decía el pobre alcaide; -
Pardon me lords said the poor warden

y yo no os ocultaré nada, siquiera sea
and I not for you hide nothing certainly (it) would be

en contra mía.
-in- against me

Todos guardaron silencio, y él prosiguió así:
All kept silent and he continued thus

- Yo no acertaré nunca a dar la razón; pero es
I not asserted never to give the reason but (it) is

el caso que la historia de las armas vacías me
the case that the story of the arms empty me
a fact   empty arms

pareció siempre una fábula tejida en favor de
seemed always a fable sewn in favor of
                        made up story

algún noble personaje, a quien tal vez altas
some noble person to whom such time high
                                    maybe (important)

razones de conveniencia pública no permitían
reasons of convenience public not permitted
                public convenience

ni descubrir ni castigar.
neither to uncover nor to punish

En esta creencia estuve siempre, creencia en que
In this believe (I) was always (a) believe in that

no podía menos de confirmarme la inmovilidad en
not could less of confirm myself the inmobility in

que se encontraban desde que por segunda vez
that itself encountered from that for second time

tornaron a la cárcel traídas del concejo. En
return to the jail brought of the council In
(by the)

vano una noche y otra, deseando sorprender su
vain one night and other desiring to surprise his

misterio, si misterio en ellas había, me levantaba
mystery if mystery in them (it) had myself (I) rose

poco a poco y aplicaba el oído a los
bit by bit and applied the hearing to the
(put) (ear)

intersticios de la ferrada puerta de su calabozo;
slits of the ironed door of his cell

ni un rumor se percibía.
not a sound itself perceived
could be perceived

En vano procuré observarlas a través de un
In vain (I) tried to observe them -to- through of a

pequeño agujero producido en el muro; arrojadas
tiny hole made in the wall thrown

sobre un poco de paja y en uno de los más
on a bit of straw and in one of the most

obscures rincones, permanecían un día y otro
dark corners (they) remained one day and other

descompuestas e inmóviles.
fallen apart and immobile

Una noche, por último, aguijoneado por la
One night for last stinged by the

curiosidad y deseando convencerme por mí
curiosity and desiring to convince myself for me

mismo de que aquel objeto de terror nada tenía
self of that that object of terror nothing had

de misterioso, encendí una linterna, bajé a las
of mysteries (I) lit a lantern went down to the

prisiones, levanté sus dobles aldabas, y no
prisons lifted its double latches and not

cuidando siquiera - tanta era mi fe en que
caring   certainly   so much was my faith in that

todo no pasaba de un cuento - de cerrar las
all   not passed of a story   of close the
    was not more than   (to)

puertas tras mí, penetré en el calabozo.
doors behind e (I) penetrated in the cell

Nunca lo hubiera hecho; apenas anduve algunos
Never it would have done hardly (I) went some

pasos, la luz de mi linterna se apagó por
steps the light of my lantern itself extinguished by

sí sola, y mis dientes comenzaron a chocar,
itself alone and my teeth started to shock
    (rattle)

y mis cabellos a erizarse. Turbando el
and my hairs to rise up -itself- Troubling the
    (hair)

profundo silencio que me rodeaba, había oído
deep silence that me surrounded (I) had heard

como un ruido de hierros, que se removían y
how a noise of irons that itself moved and

chocaban al unirse
crashed at the joining itself

entre   las sombras.
between the shadows

Mi   primer movimiento fue arrojarme   a   la
My   first   movement   was to throw myself to   the

puerta para cerrar el   paso, pero al   asir   sus
door   to   close   the pass   but   at the   to grab my

hojas,   sentí sobre mis hombros   una
sheets   felt   on   my   shoulders a

mano formidable – cubierta con   un guantelete, que
hand formidable   covered   with a   gauntlet   that
      big hand

después de   sacudirme con   violencia me
after   -of- to jolt me with violence   me

derribó   sobre el   dintel. Allí   permanecí   hasta
knocked down over   the lintel   There (she) remained until

la   mañana   siguiente, que   me encontraron mis
the morning next   that me encountered my
     next morning   me found

servidores falto   de sentido, y   recordando sólo
servants   wanting   of sense   and remembering only
                          senseless

que después de mi caída, había creído percibir
that after of my fall (I) had believed to perceive

confusamente como unas pisadas sonoras, al
confusedly like some steps sounding at the

compás de las cuales resonaba un rumor de
measure of the which resounded a rumor of

espuelas, que poco a poco se fue alejando
spurs that little by little themselves were moving away

hasta perderse.
until to lose themselves
(they were silent)

Cuando concluyó el alcaide, reinó un
When concluded the warden reigned a

silencio profundo, al que siguió luego un
silence deep at the that followed after an
deep silence

infernal concierto de lamentaciones, gritos y
infernal concert of lamentations screams and

amenazas.
threats

Trabajo costó a los más pacificos el contener
Work   cost to the most peaceful (one) the containing
It was difficult for   to contain

al pueblo que, furioso con la novedad, pedía a
to the people that furious with the novelty asked at
(of the)

grandes voces la muerte del curioso autor de su
great voices the death of the curious author of its

nueva desgracia.
new disgrace

Al cabo logróse apaciguar el tumulto,
At the end (he) achieved himself to pacify the tumult
              (he managed)

y comenzaron a disponerse a una nueva
and (they) started to dispose themselves to a new
                (set off)

persecución. Ésta obtuvo también un
persecution This obtained also a

resultado satisfactorio.
result satisfactory
satisfactory result

Al cabo de algunos días, la armadura volvió a
At the end of some days the armor returned to

encontrarse en poder de sus perseguidores.
encounter itself in power of his persecutors
(be found)

Conocida la fórmula, y mediante la ayuda de
Known the formula and through the help of

San Bartolomé, la cosa no era ya muy difícil.
San Bartolome the thing not was already very difficult
already was not

Pero aún quedaba algo por hacer: pues en
But still remained something -for- to do since in

vano, a fin de sujetarlo, lo colgaron de una
vain at end of secure it it hung from a
to

horca; en vano emplearon la más exquisita
gallow(s) in vain employed the most exquisite

vigilancia con el objeto de quitarle toda
vigilance with the object of to take away of him all

ocasión de escaparse por esos mundos. En
opportunity of to escape for those worlds In
to another world

cuanto las desunidas armas veían dos dedos de
how much the disunited arms saw two fingers of
fallen apart armor

luz, se encajaban, y pian pianito, volvían a
light themselves caged and slow slowly returned to
were locked in

tomar el trote y emprender de nuevo sus
take the trot and undertake of new its
again

excursiones por montes y llanos, que era una
excursions by mountains and flats that was a

bendición del cielo.
blessing of the sky

Aquello era el cuento de nunca acabar.
That was the story of never to finish

En tan angustiosa situación, los vecinos se
In such (an) anxious situation the neighbors themselves

repartieron entre sí las piezas de la armadura,
divided between them the pieces of the armor

que acaso por la centésima vez
that maybe for the hundredth time

se encontraba en sus manos, y rogando
themselves encountered in their hands and demanding
was found

al piadoso eremita, que un día los iluminó
at the pious hermit lady that one day them (he) illuminated

con sus consejos, decidiera lo que debía hacerse
with his councils decided it that must do
                                                       that which

de ella.
of her
(with){the armor}

El santo varón ordenó al pueblo una
The holy man ordered -to- the people a

penitencia general. Se encerré por tres días en
penitence generic Himself enclosed for three days in

el fondo de una caverna que le servía de asilo,
the depth of a cavern that him served as refuge

y al cabo de ellos dispuso que se
and at the end of these (days) disposed that themselves
                                                    (decided)

fundiesen las diabólicas armas, y con ellas y
melt the devilish arms and with them and
                                    (armor)

algunos sillares del castillo del Segre, se
some ashlars of the castle of the Segre themselves

levantase una cruz.
erect a cross

La operación se llevó a término, aunque no
The operation itself took to end although not

sin que nuevos y aterradores prodigios
without that new and terrifying prodigies

llenasen de pavor el ánimo de los
filled themselves of fear the spirit of the

consternados habitantes de Bellver.
dismayed inhabitants of Bellver

En tanto que las piezas arrojadas a las llamas
In so much that the pieces thrown at the flames

comenzaban a enrojecerse, largos y profundos
started to redden themselves large and deep

gemidos parecían escaparse de la ancha
groans seemed to escape themselves from the wide

hoguera, de entre cuyos troncos saltaban como
bonfire of between whose trunks jumped out as

si estuvieran vivas y sintiesen la acción del
if (they) were alive and felt the action of the

fuego. Una tromba de chispas rojas, verdes y
fire A whirlwind of sparks red green and

azules danzaba en la cúspide de sus encendidas
blue danced in the cusp of their lit (flaming)

lenguas, y se retorcían crujiendo como si
tongues and themselves writhed creaking as if

una legión de diablos, cabalgando sobre ellas,
an army of devils riding on them

pugnasen por libertar a su señor de aquel
were battling -for- to free -to- their master of that

tormento.
torment

Extraña, horrible fue la operación, en tanto que
Strange horrible was the operation in so much that

la candente armadura perdía su forma para tomar
the glowing armor lost its form for to take

la   de una cruz.
that   of   a   cross

Los   martillos, caían   resonando   con   un   espantoso
The   hammers   falling   resounding   with   a   frightful

estruendo   sobre   el   yunque,   al   que   veinte
din   on   the   anvil   at the   that   twenty
                                         while

trabajadores   vigorosos   sujetaban   las   barras   del
workers   vigorous   subjected   the   bars   of the

hirviente   metal,   que   palpitaba   y   gemía
boiling   metal   that   throbbed   and   moaned

al   sentir los golpes.
at the   to feel   the   blows
   at feeling

Ya   se   extendían los brazos   del   signo de
Already   themselves   extended   the   arms   of the   sign   of

nuestra   redención,   ya   comenzaba   a   formarse
our   redemption   already   started   to   form itself

la   cabecera,   cuando   la   diabólica   y   encendida
the   headboard   when   the   diabolic   and   lit

masa   se   retorcía   de nuevo   como   en   una
mass   itself   twisted   of   new   like   in   a
     again

convulsión   espantosa,   y   rodeándose   al
convulsion   frightening   and   surrounding themselves   at the

cuerpo   de   los   desgraciados,   que   pugnaban   por
corps   of   the   unfortunate ones   that   battled   for

desasirse   de   sus   brazos   de   muerte,   se
free themselves   of   its   arms   of   death   itself

enroscaba   en   anillas   como   una   culebra,   o   se
coiled   in   rings   like   a   snake   or   itself

contraía   en   zigzag   como   un   relámpago.
contracted   in   zigzag   like   a   lightning

El   constante   trabajo,   la   fe,   las   oraciones   y   el
The   constant   work   the   faith   the   prayers   and   the

agua   bendita   consiguieron,   por   último,   vencer
water   blessed   succeeded   for   last   to overcome
   blessed water   (at)

el   espíritu   infernal   y   la   armadura   se   convirtió
the   spirit   infernal   and   the   armor   itself   converted

en cruz.
in (a) cross

Esa cruz es la que hoy habéis visto, y a la
That cross is that what today (you) have seen and at the

cual se encuentra sujeto el diablo que le
which itself encountered subject the devil that her

presta su nombre; ante ella, ni las jóvenes
borrows its name before her neither the youths

colocan en el mes de Mayo ramilletes de lirios,
place in the month of May corsages of lilies

ni los pastores se descubren al pasar, ni
nor the shepherds themselves uncover at the to pass nor
take off their hats

los ancianos se arrodillan, bastando apenas
the old people themselves kneel down being enough hardly

las severas amonestaciones del clero para que los
the severe admonishments of the clergy for that the

muchachos no la apedreen.
boys not her pelt with stones

Dios — God
ha — has
cerrado — closed
sus — his
oídos — ears
a — to
cuantas — so much
plegarias — prayers

se — themselves
le — her
dirijan — (they) say
en — in
su — her
presencia. — presence
En — In
el — the

invierno — winter
los — the
lobos — wolves
se — themselves
reúnen — reunite
en — in
manadas — packs

junto — together
al — at the
enebro — juniper
que — that
la — her
protege, — protects
para — for

lanzarse — to launch themselves
sobre — on
las — the
reses; — cattle
los — the
bandidos — bandits

esperan — wait
a — at
su — her
sombra — shadow
a — at
los — the
caminantes, — travelers
que — that

entierran — (they) bury
a — at
su — her
pie — foot
después — after
que — that
los — them
asesinan; — (they) murder
y — and

cuando — when
la — the
tempestad — storm
se — itself
desata, — unleashes
los — the
rayos — rays

tuercen — twist
su — their
camino — road
para — for
liarse, — to link themselves
silbando, — whistling

al   asta de esa cruz y romper los sillares de
at the   shaft of that cross and break the ashlars of

su pedestal.
her pedestal

LAS HOJAS SECAS

LAS HOJAS SECAS
The   Leaves   Dry
The Dry Leaves

El   sol   se   había   puesto: las   nubes,   que
The   sun   -itself-   had   set   the   clouds   that

cruzaban   hechas   jirones   sobre   mi   cabeza,   iban   a
crossed   made   wisps   over   my   head   went   to
(came over)

amontonarse   unas   sobre   otras   en   el
pile themselves   ones   on   (the) others   on   the

horizonte   lejano.   El   viento   frío   de   las   tardes   de
horizon   distant   The   wind   cold   of   the   afternoons   of
distant horizon

otoño   arremolinaba   las   hojas   secas   a   mis   pies.
autumn   swirled   the   leaves   dry   at   my   feet

Yo   estaba   sentado   al   borde   de   un   camino,   por
I   was   seated   at the   edge   of   a   road   for

donde siempre vuelven menos de los que van.
where always return less of those that go
(than)

No sé en qué pensaba, si en efecto pensaba
Not (I) know on what (I) thought if in effect (I) thought

entonces en alguna cosa. Mi alma temblaba a
then on any thing My soul trembled at

punto de lanzarse al espacio, como el pájaro
point of to launch itself to the space like the bird

tiembla y agita ligeramente las alas antes de
trembles and moves slightly the wings before of

levantar el vuelo.
to pick up the flight

Hay momentos en que, merced a una serie de
Has moments in that thanks to a series of
(There are)

abstracciones, el espíritu se sustrae a cuanto
abstractions the spirit itself subtracts to how much

le rodea, y replegándose en sí mismo analiza
it surrounds and falling back itself on itself self analyses

y
and

comprende todos los misteriosos fenómenos de la
comprehends all the mysterious phenomenons of the

vida interna del hombre.
life internal of the human

Hay otros en que se desliga de la carne,
Has others in that itself (it) unbinds from the flesh
(There are)

pierde su personalidad y se confunde con los
looses its personality and itself mixes with the

elementos de la naturaleza, se relaciona con su
elements of the nature itself relates with her

modo de ser, y traduce su incomprensible
manner of to see and translates her incomprehensible

lenguaje.
language

Yo me hallaba en uno de estos últimos
I myself found in one of these last

momentos, cuando solo y en medio de la
moments when only and in half of the

escueta llanura, oí hablar cerca de mí.
bare   plain   (I) Heard   talk   close   of   me

Eran dos hojas secas las que hablaban, y
(They) were   two   leaves   dry   those   that   talked   and

éste, poco más o menos, su extraño diálogo:
this   (a) bit   more   or   less   their   strange   dialogue

- ¿De dónde vienes, hermana?
From   where   come (you)   sister

- Vengo de rodar con el torbellino, envuelta en
(I) come   from   to roll   with   the   whirlwind   enveloped   in

la nube del polvo y de las hojas secas nuestras
the   cloud   of the   dust   and   of   the   leaves   dry   our

compañeras, a lo largo de la interminable llanura.
companions   at   the   length   of   the   unending   plain

¿Y tú?
And   you

- Yo he seguido algún tiempo la corriente del
I   have   followed   some   time   the   stream   of the

río, hasta que el vendaval me arrancó de entre
river until that the gale me tore from between

el légamo y los juncos de la orilla.
the slime and the rushes of the shore
  (mud)

- ¿Y adónde vas?
And where go (you)

- No lo sé: ¿lo sabe acaso el viento que me
Not it (I) know It knows maybe the wind that me

empuja?
pushes

- ¡Ay! ¿Quién diría que habíamos de acabar
Ay Who shall say that (we) had of to end

amarillas y secas arrastrándonos por la tierra,
yellow and dry dragging ourselves on the ground

nosotras que vivimos vestidas de color y de luz
us that live dressed of color and of light

meciéndonos en el aire?
swaying ourselves in the air

- ¿Te acuerdas de los hermosos días en que
You remember of the beautiful days in that

brotamos; de aquella apacible mañana en que,
(we) sprouted of that peaceful morning in that

roto el hinchado botón que nos servía de
(once) broken the swollen bud that us served of
(as)

cuna, nos desplegamos al templado beso
cradle ourselves unfolded to the mild kiss

del sol como un abanico de esmeraldas?
of the sun like a fan of emeralds

- ¡Oh! ¡Qué dulce era sentirse balanceada por
Oh What sweet was (it) to feel oneself swung by
(How)

la brisa a aquella altura, bebiendo por todos
the breeze at that height drinking through all

los poros el aire y la luz!
the pores the air and the light

- ¡Oh! ¡Qué hermoso era ver correr el agua
Oh What beautiful (it) was to see run the water
(How)

del río que lamía las retorcidas raíces del
of the river that lapped the twisted roots of the

añoso tronco que nos sustentaba, aquel agua
yearful trunk that us sustained that water
(old)

limpia y trasparente que copiaba como un espejo
clean and transparent that copied like a mirror

el azul del cielo, de modo que creíamos vivir
the blue of the sky of manner that (we) believed to live

suspendidas entre dos abismos azules!
suspended between two abysses blue

- ¡Con qué placer nos asomábamos por cima
With what pleasure ourselves peeped ourselves by top

de las verdes frondas para vernos retratadas
of the green foliage for to see ourselves portrayed

en la temblorosa corriente!
in the trembling stream
(flickering)

- ¡Cómo cantábamos juntas imitando el rumor
How (we) sang ourselves together imitating the sound

de la brisa y siguiendo el ritmo de las ondas!
of the wind and following the rhythm of the waves

- Los insectos brillantes revoloteaban desplegando
The insects shining fluttered unfolding

sus alas de gasa a nuestro alrededor.
their wings of gauze at our vicinity

- Y las mariposas blancas y las libélulas azules,
And the butterflies white and the dragonflies blue

que giran por el aire en extraños círculos,
that gyrated through the air in strange circles

se paraban un momento en nuestros
themselves stopped a moment on our

dentellados bordes a contarse los secretos de
teethed edges to tell each other the secrets of
(serrated)

ese misterioso amor que dura un instante y les
that mysterious love that takes an instant and them

consume la vida.
consumes the life

- Cada cual de nosotras era una nota en el
Each which of ours was a note in the
(one)

concierto de los bosques.
concert of the forests

- Cada cual de nosotras era un tono en la
Each which of ours was a tone in the
(one)

armonía de su color.
harmony of its color

- En las noches de luna, cuando su plateada luz
In the nights of moon when its silver light
moonlit nights

resbalaba sobre la cima de los montes, ¿te
slid over the top of the mountains yourself

acuerdas cómo charlábamos en voz baja entre
(you) remember how (we) chatted in voice low between

las diáfanas sombras?
the diaphanous shadows
(transparent)

- Y referíamos con un blando susurro las
And (we) referred with a soft whisper the

historias de los silfos que se columpian en
histories of the sylphs that themselves swung in

los hilos de oro que cuelgan las arañas entre los
the threads of gold that hung the spiders between the

árboles.
trees

- Hasta que suspendíamos nuestra monótona
Until that (we) suspended our monotonous

charla para oír embebecidas las quejas del
chat for to listen imbibed the complains of the

ruiseñor, que había escogido nuestro tronco por
nightingale that had chosen our trunk for

escabel.
footstool

- Y eran tan tristes y tan suaves sus lamentos
And were so sad and so gentle his laments

que, aunque llenas de gozo al oírle,
*that although full of joy at the to hear it
when hearing it*

nos amanecía llorando.
us   (it) dawned   crying
us saw crying in the morning

- ¡Oh! ¡Qué dulces eran aquellas lágrimas que nos
  Oh   What   sweet   were   those   tears   that us
  (How)

prestaba el   rocío de   la   noche y   que
loaned   the dew   of   the night and that

resplandecían con todos los colores del   iris a
glittered   with all   the colors   of the rainbow at
                                                   {arco iris}

la primera luz de la aurora!
the first   light of the aurora
                         (sunrise)

- Después vino la alegre banda de jilgueros a
  After   came the merry   band   of goldfinches to

llenar de vida y de ruidos el bosque con la
fill   of life and of sounds of (the) forest with the
(with)   (with)

alborozada y confusa algarabía de sus cantos.
exhilarated and confused hubbub   of their songs

- Y una enamorada pareja, colgó junto a
  And an   in love   pair   hung   next   to

nosotras su redondo nido de aristas y de
us their round nest of beard (of grain) and of

plumas.
feathers

- Nosotras servíamos de abrigo a los pequeñuelos
Ourselves (we) served of shelter to the small ones
(as)

contra las molestas gotas de la lluvia en las
against the molesting drops of the rain in the

tempestades de verano.
tempests of summer

- Nosotras les servíamos de dosel y los
Ourselves them (we) served of canopy and them
(as)

defendíamos de los importunos rayos del sol.
(we) defended from the importune rays of the sun

- Nuestra vida pasaba como un sueño de oro, del
Our life passed like a dream of gold of it

que no sospechábamos que se podría
that not (we) suspected that oneself (one) could

despertar.
wake up

\- Una   hermosa   tarde   en   que   todo   parecía
  A   beautiful   afternoon   in   that   all   seemed

sonreír   a   nuestro   alrededor,   en   que   el   sol
to smile   at   our   surroundings   in   that   the   sun

poniente   encendía   el   ocaso   y   arrebolaba   las
setting   set on fire   the   twilight   and   made glow   the

nubes,   y   de   la   tierra   ligeramente   húmeda   se
clouds   and   from   the   ground   lightly   humid   itself

levantaban   efluvios   de   vida   y   perfumes   de
lifted   outpourings   of   life   and   perfumes   of

flores,   dos   amantes   se   detuvieron   a   la   orilla
flowers   two   lovers   themselves   stopped   at   the   shore

del   agua   y   al   pie   del   tronco   que   nos
of the   water   and   at the   foot   of the   trunk   that   us

sostenía.
sustained

- ¡Nunca se borrará ese recuerdo de mi
Never itself will erase that recollection from my

memoria! Ella era joven, casi una niña, hermosa
memory She was young almost a girl beautiful

y pálida. Él le decía con ternura: - ¿Por qué
and pale He her said with tenderness For what

lloras? - Perdona este involuntario sentimiento
do (you) cry Pardon this involuntary sentiment

de egoísmo, le respondió ella enjugándose una
of egoism him responded she wiping of herself a

lágrima; lloro por mí. Lloro la vida que me huye:
tear (I) cry for me (I) cry the life that me flees

cuando el cielo se corona de rayos de luz, y
when the sky itself crowns of rays of light and
(with)

la tierra se viste de verdura y de flores, y
the earth itself dresses of green and of flowers and
(with) (with)

el viento trae perfumes y cantos de pájaros
the wind carries perfumes and songs of (the) birds

115

y armonías distantes, y se ama y se
and harmonies far away and oneself loves and oneself

siente una amada ¡la vida es buena! - ¿Y por qué
feels one loved the life is good And for what

no has de vivir? insistió él estrechándole las
not (you) have of to live insisted he grasping of her the

manos conmovido. - Porque es imposible. Cuando
hands touched Because (it) is impossible When

caigan secas - esas hojas que murmuran
fall dry those leaves that murmur

armoniosas sobre nuestras cabezas, yo moriré
harmonious over our heads I will die

también, y el viento llevará algún día su polvo
as well and the wind will carry some day your dust

y el mío ¿quién sabe adónde?
and the mine who knows where

- Yo lo oí y tú lo oíste, y nos estremecimos
I it heard and you it heard and we shivered

y callamos. ¡Debíamos secarnos! ¡Debíamos
and became silent (We) must dry ourselves (We) must

morir y girar arrastradas por los remolinos del
die and gyrate torn by the whirls of the

viento! Mudas y llenas de terror permanecíamos
wind Mute and filled of terror (we) remained

aun cuando llegó la noche. ¡Oh!
still when arrived the night Oh

¡Qué noche tan horrible!
What night so horrible
What a horrible night

- Por la primera vez faltó a su cita el
For the first time lacked at its place the

enamorado ruiseñor que la encantaba con sus
enamored nightingale that her enchanted with its

quejas.
complaints

- A poco volaron los pájaros, y con ellos sus
At little flew the birds and with them their

pequeñuelos   ya   vestidos   de   plumas;   y   quedó
little ones   already   dressed   of   feathers   and   remained

el   nido   solo,   columpiándose   lentamente   y   triste,
the   nest   alone   swinging itself   slowly   and   sadly

como   la   cuna   vacía   de   un   niño   muerto.
like   the   cradle   empty   of   a   child   dead

-    Y   huyeron   las   mariposas   blancas   y   las
And   fled   the   butterflies   white   and   the

libélulas   azules,   dejando   su   lugar   a   los   insectos
dragonflies   blue   leaving   their   place   to   the   insects

obscuros   que   venían   a   roer   nuestras   fibras   y   a
dark   that   came   to   gnaw   our   fibers   and   to

depositar   en   nuestro   seno   sus   asquerosas   larvas.
deposit   in   our   breast   their   disgusting   larvae

- ¡Oh!   ¡Y   cómo   nos   estremecíamos   encogidas
Oh   And   how   ourselves   (we) shivered   shrunken

al   helado   contacto   de   las   escarchas   de   la
at the   frozen   contact   of   the   hoarfrosts   of   the

noche!
night

- Perdimos el color y la frescura.
(We) lost the color and the freshness

- Perdimos la suavidad y las formas, y lo que
(We) lost the tenderness and the forms and that what

antes al tocarnos era como rumor de
before at the touching ourselves was like rumor of
(touching each other)

besos, como murmullo de palabras de enamorados,
kisses like murmur of words of loved ones

luego se convirtió en áspero ruido, seco,
after itself converted in rough noise dry

desagradable y triste.
disagreeable and sad

- ¡Y al fin volamos desprendidas!
And at the end (we) flew coming away

- Hollada bajo el pie de indiferente pasajero,
Trodden under the foot of (an) indifferent passer by

sin   cesar arrastrada de un punto a otro
without   stop   dragged   from one point to (an)other

entre el polvo y el fango, me he juzgado
between the dust and the mud myself (I) have judged

dichosa cuando podía reposar un instante en el
lucky when (I) could rest an instant in the

profundo surco de un camino.
deep groove of a road

- Yo he dado vueltas sin cesar arrastrada por
I have given turns without stop dragged by

la turbia corriente, y en mi larga peregrinación
the turbulent stream and in my large pilgrimage

vi, solo, enlutado y sombrío, contemplando
(I) saw alone in mourning and somber contemplating

con una mirada distraída las aguas que pasaban
with a glance distracted the waters that passed

y las hojas secas que marcaban su movimiento,
and the leaves dry that marked its movement

a   uno de los dos amantes cuyas palabras nos
-to- one of the two lovers whose words us

hicieron presentir la muerte.
made present -the- death

- ¡Ella también se desprendió de la vida y
  She as well herself detached from the life and

acaso dormirá en una fosa reciente, sobre la
maybe will sleep in a hollow fresh on which

que yo me detuve un momento!
that I myself stop a moment

- ¡Ay! Ella duerme y reposa al fin; ¿pero
  Ai She sleeps and rests to the end but

nosotras, cuando acabaremos este largo viaje?...
us when do (we) finish this long journey

- ¡Nunca!... Ya el viento que nos dejó reposar
  Never Already the wind that us let rest

un punto vuelve a soplar, y ya me siento
a point returns to blow and already me (I) feel

estremecida para levantarme de la tierra y
shook to lift myself from the ground and

seguir con él. ¡Adiós, hermana!
continue with it Goodbye sister

- ¡Adiós!...
Goodbye

Silbó el aire que había permanecido un
Whistled the air that had remained (for) a

momento callado, y las hojas se levantaron
moment silent and the leaves themselves rose

en confuso remolino, perdiéndose a lo lejos
in confused swirl loosing themselves at the distance

entre las tinieblas de la noche.
between the darkness of the night

Y yo pensé entonces algo que no puedo
And I thought then something that not (I) can

recordar, y que, aunque lo recordase, no
remember and that even if it (I) remember not

encontraría palabras para decirlo.
(I) would find   words   for   to tell it

www.ingramcontent.com/pod-product-compliance
Lightning Source LLC
LaVergne TN
LVHW011334080426
835513LV00006B/346